This Is My Story
AN AUTOBIOGRAPHY

WILLIAM RICHARD IKNER, SR.

This Is My Story:

An Autobiography

William Richard Ikner, Sr.

Copyright © 2021 by Monarch Educational Services, LLC.

William Richard Ikner, Sr. left his autobiography and it was found after death. This is his life story as he saw fit to tell it, and written in his words. Dr. Jennifer Lowry (daughter of William Richard Ikner, Sr.) published this book in his memory, for the sole purposes of honoring his life and that of his family. No harm was intended in publishing this book. Any mention of names, events, places, settings, and situations in the book were solely penned by William Richard Ikner, Sr.

All pictures were provided by Jennifer Ikner Lowry, daughter of William Richard Ikner, Sr.

All proceeds from book sales will be donated to charity. Please visit the Children of Fallen Heroes website to learn more about the organization: https://www.childrenoffallenheroes.org/

All rights reserved.

No part of this book may be reproduced in any form or by any electronic or mechanical means, including information storage and retrieval systems, without written permission from the publisher, except for the use of brief quotations in a book review.

Dedicated to my lovely wife Betty Lou and children

Introduction

We would like to thank you for what you are about to do. You are about to read the story of a strong, loving husband, father, grandfather, and friend. You may not know him. You may have never heard of Bill "The Rock" Ikner or Billy or William or Buzzard or the other names we may not even know about. We were blessed to have him in our lives for the time the Lord gave us. We are thankful to have his words, these very words that are typed in these pages, to carry on his memory, his stories, and his life.

William Richard Ikner, Sr. served faithfully in the United States Army. He does discuss horrific details of his time at Desert Rock and tours during Vietnam. War is not pretty. Neither is what he describes in his life story.

If you are looking for perfect grammar, don't. If you are looking for proper sentence structure or wondering how we could print words without an editor, then remember that we are capturing his life story that was written by him for us. This is his autobiography, typed to share his life in his very manner of speaking. It is him in every way. We love every single word that he left for us. We pray you love it, too. Unfiltered. Unchecked. Real.

INTRODUCTION

Thank you for reading his story and sharing a part of his history, our history, for a little while. May he be resting in the arms of Jesus.

This Is My Story

At the time of my birth, June 21, 1935, America was still in a depression and life for a poor family was very hard. My mother, Ellen Gertrude Rasberry, and Carl Woodrow Ikner got married on November 10, 1934. Mom was only 13 years old and Dad was 22 years old. My dad came from a very large family, 19 children.

Monroe and Rosanne Davis Ikner were married in 1904 and raised their family on the family farm, raising and growing most of their needs. In the family line, I don't remember where Dad was, but I think he was one of the first five children they had. Monroe and Rosanne lived their entire lives in Columbus County, NC. Rosa gave birth to eighteen children and later adopted one. Monroe owned his own farm and raised his children to know the value of a hard days work. Monroe was married three times in his span of life. His second wife was Emma and Ida, his third.

Monroe and Rosa had three of their children die at an early age: Maybelle, Maggie, and Robert. The rest of the children have all married except Dock, who chose to remain single. The children were: Tom, Pete, Re Walter, Woodrow, Junior, Eugene, Dock, David, Robert, Elnita, Alma, Macie, Olean, Dorothy, Louise, Brenda, Maybelle, and Maggie.

Before Monroe passed, he sold his old home place and moved to the Cypress Creek area. Not only did Monroe have a great love for his family, but also for the Lord. (He built his own church on his property to worship. He lived a long and a well productive life leaving a long line of descendants to carry on the name Ikner.

I know Dad had married another woman before mom but it was annulled after a couple of days. He finished high school and loved to play baseball in school, and he also loved boxing. He did really well until he quit to get married. I believe it was called *Golden Glove Boxing* and once he fought for the lightweight championship in Raleigh, but he told me the guy he fought had a fist made of steel.

About the only thing available for work at that time was working in a store or farming. Dad said he was not out to be a store clerk so when he and mom were married they got a shanty shack of a house on the John Conduit farm and sharecropped with him several years making just enough money to survive. Mom said that the old house had so many holes in the roof you could count the stars at night and get wet when it rained and nearly froze in the winter, but it was all they could get so they had to make out with it. Mom said the owners were good to them, giving them plenty of milk, eggs, and they had a small garden to raise some food. The Conduits didn't have any children but she loved cats, and mom said she had sometimes as many as thirty in her house. Mom said when she would give her cooked food she would have to check it to make sure there were no cat hairs in it.

The Conduit farm was about three miles from Whiteville and Dad would have to walk to town to buy groceries. Like flour, sugar, and coffee, whatever they could afford. It was in the New Hope community and they had a school, a church, and a small country store. Mom said working on a farm back then was really hard work. Tobacco, corn, and oats were the main crops, but mules were used to do the fieldwork. Mom finished the fifth grade in school. She had to help with her brother and sisters plus work in the fields so she knew what hard work was. She had two sisters, Flora Bell and Shelby, and two brothers, Sam and one adopted brother named Jerry. Evelyn died when she was about sixteen years old with Spinal Meningitis.

Mom learned how to cook and take care of a house at a really early age. She told me once she didn't clean the old wood stove the way that Grandma wanted it and she got a beating. That was when her and Dad were dating and she said it really did embarrass her because she got beat when he was at her house. Grandma believed in a clean house at all times.

I don't know when Sam Montgomery Rasberry and Lela Sikes were married but Mom was born June 20, 1921. She was their first child. Then there was Flora Bell, Sam Montgomery Jr., Shelby Jean, and Jerry Lynn (adopted). Granddad, Sam was what he was called, was a very hard working father, and he sharecropped with larger farmers all his life. He was born poor, and he died poorer. He was a wonderful father and did only what he knew best for his family. He never had a driving license or owned a vehicle. A mule and wagon was his mode of travel. He was never ashamed of what he did, and his family never went without a shelter over their head, food on the table, or clothes on their backs.

So, when Mom and Dad got married they knew it would be hard to make it, but together they did. They raised four wonderful children, myself (William Richard Ikner), Rosa Lee, Carl Floyd, and Annette. And in March 1987, the Lord called Dad, and December 27, 1997, He called mom.

Ellen Gertrude and Woodrow Ikner (Billy's parents), 1955

I remember Mom telling me about my younger days. Whiteville opened a new hospital the week I was born. A girl was the first baby born and I was the first boy. Mom always told me I was born on her birthday, June 20, 1935, but when I got my birth certificate, it had me born on the 21st. Mom said the doctor just signed the certificate a day later, and she knew I was born on the 20th.

Mom said I was raised on fresh cow's milk. I guess that is why I love milk so much. She said that it was hard that summer because she had to work in tobacco and take care of me also, but she managed to do it. She also told me about the milk. She would have to boil it and strain it to make sure that there were no cat hairs in it. (I guess that might be why I can't stand cats today.) Mom also told me about hiding my toys if other kids came to the house.

Mom said she got her first real scare when I was about 22 months old. I can't remember who came to the house now, but mom said they were driving a T. Model car and me and the other kids were running around the car and the running board had a very sharp edge in one area and I fell and hit my head and it put a 2 inch gash. I was bleeding really hard and they had to carry me to the hospital. I still have the scar today.

The next time I was about three and a half years old and they had moved to the Walter Butler farm in the same area. Mom said Dad had finished curing a barn of tobacco and had taken the ashes out of the furnace to cool and had told her he was going to the store to pick up some items. Mom was outside cleaning the yard, and I was with her. She said she thought I was playing but I had tried to follow Dad, and she heard me hollering. The tobacco barn was about 100 yards from the house. She said she started running to the barn and that I was standing in a pile of hot ashes, screaming. She grabbed me out of the ashes and started running to the store with me screaming. There were some folks at the store who had an old truck and he drove us to the hospital. My small feet had been cooked. Mom said it was over a year before I could walk again without hurting.

I remember her talking about the house we lived in when this happened. She said it was a little better but now Rosa Lee was a baby. She said that they had a hard time keeping the snakes out of the house, especially during the cold months. And the bears liked to come into the yard looking for food. She said back then they didn't have locks on the doors. Just slide bolts and she would pray the bears wouldn't figure it out or break the doors down. There was no electricity, running water or inside bathrooms.

I know that we would move to the Laurel Hill area after the crops were in but Dad would go back to Whiteville in time for spring crop planting. Mom said we once lived at Sandy Bottom, where Bobby Clark's junkyard is today. It was a converted hotel about a 12 by 12 building.

I remember starting school when I was six years old at New Hope School, south of Whiteville, NC. Mom said she walked me to school, about half a mile and about two hours later I was back home. She asked me what I was doing at home and I told her I was thirsty and came home for some water. As you would guess, she took me back to school and showed me where to go for water and the inside bathroom. I didn't stay there long but I do remember a lot of us boys got a got a beating for pushing one of the boys into a large ditch which was almost full of water. After all the crops were tended, we headed back to Ida Mill, NC.

We shared a four-room house with another family, Sheppard's, Jewel's parents. I also remember one year we lived in the old two-story house at Ida Mill and Red Campbell and his family shared it with us. Ida Mill was a mill village but we had a store, a church, and one house had an old telephone on the porch so anyone could use it if needed. Us kids knew we were not to touch it.

At this time, Carl (Shotgun) was a baby. There were five of us. One room was the bedroom. It had two double beds, and the other was the kitchen. The small porch is where the hand pump was located and the outdoor toilet had two holes, that way we could use it at the same time. We stayed here for several years. Annette came along while we lived there, so that made six of us still in two rooms.

I have a few memories of those years. Laurel Hill was about a mile away and we had to walk to school there. The railroad was on the way so that was generally our path to and from school. There were quite a few kids living at Ida Mill so there was always a group walking to school, rain or shine, cold or hot. We were still taking baths in large tubs. I think I was ten years old before I ever took a bath in an inside bathroom or lived in a house with all the plumbing.

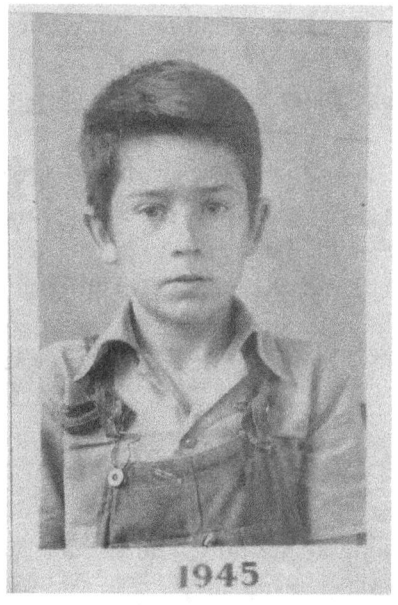

Billy Ikner, Age 10

Everyone who lived at Ida Mill worked for Morgan Mills. The folks worked hard during the week but on the weekends, the moonshine liquor poured like water. A lot of the men played musical instruments and on Saturday night, there was usually plenty of picking and singing. Dad could play the guitar a little but he lost his middle finger in an accident at the mill so to be able to join in he built himself a washboard. It was made of a large washboard, the turntable on a record player, a cowbell, and squeeze horn. He could play it real good. He used metal thimbles on the fingers. There were guitars, banjos, fiddles, dobro guitars, bass fiddle, steel guitar, drums and dad's washboard.

They could really play when they got about three sheets in the wind (half drunk). But then on Sunday morning the little church would be full. I remember once Annette got really sick and there was no one around who could carry her to the Laurinburg hospital. Mom said her eyes had rolled back in their sockets and were set. Mom thought that she was dead. The furniture man from *Rhode's Furniture* drove up on the Mill Hill, and one of the women got him to drive mom and Annette to the hospital. Dad was at work and they called the mill in Laurinburg, #6, and told him. I don't remember what was wrong with Annette but she recovered.

Another incident I remember was the time Rosa Lee had taken some medicine. When mom got home, I told her but I didn't know what she had taken. We had a large fenced area for our chickens. Mom tried to get Rosa Lee to tell her what she had taken, but Rosa Lee wouldn't tell her, so mom got a switch and started chasing Rosa Lee around and around the chicken fence until she (Mom) was tired. So, she sent me to catch her and bring her back to her. Mom really put a beating on Rosa Lee for running.

At this time, a lot of Ikners lived in the Mill Village, Pete and William, Rue and Janice, and us. Later Walter and Betty moved there also. I remember Dad had bought him a 1939 Plymouth car and that's how they got to and from work. I remembered when Mom worked second shift, one of the ... girls would watch after us. Mom tried to work the first shift as much as possible because of us kids.

Once Dad was on the way home on Saturday night and I guess they had stopped for a few beers. He had three guys riding home with him. Coming down West Church Street there was a really sharp curve and Dad was driving too fast and he hit the large oak tree and messed the front of his car up really bad but he was able to drive on to Ida Mill. I remember him and mom fussing a lot because of his drinking and not long after that Mom loaded all of us kids on the bus and we went to live with Grandpa Rasberry for a few days until Dad came and Mom decided to go back with him. He didn't drink much for a long time after that. I guess he was afraid Mom would leave him for good.

I also remember once Uncle Junior came to the house, and he had a woman with him and he said they were married. Mom put us kids at night on a quilt in the kitchen. Junior was supposed to be looking for work but he never would go looking. So, he would watch us kids while Mom and Dad worked. Well, one day he begged Dad to let him use his car and Dad finally gave in. Dad had it fixed from the tree collision. Well, Junior and the woman loaded us kids in the car and we went toward Laurinburg, but right above Elmore's Crossroad there was a store that sold beer. So, that was where they stopped. They told us to stay in the car and that they would be back out soon. I remember it was very dark when they came back out and he was going to have to hurry and get us home so he could go get Mom, Dad, and the others from Laurinburg. Well, when he went to turn off the road to go to the house, he ran in the ditch and messed up the front end of the car again. He told us not to tell them that they had been to the beer joint. Well, you know how kids are and the next day Junior and the woman left and they never did come back to stay with us again. Dad later found out that they were not married.

The third near death happened while we were at Ida Mill. The neighbor who lived in front of us, (I believe Brooks), had some children also and one of the boys and I were good friends. One day they gave the boy some money and told him he could go to Laurel Hill at *Pate's* and buy himself a new overall jacket to wear to school. He asked me to go with him and Mom said it would be ok. Well, he got the jacket with the big brass buttons on the front and we started walking back to the house and when we got down to the railroad tracks the furniture truck from *Rhode's* was stopped and the driver was talking to someone. We asked him if he would give us a ride to Ida Mill and he said he was not stopping there.

Well, while he was talking we figured he was not telling the truth so we positioned ourselves on the bumper and it was sure sharp. He finally drove off not knowing we were on the back.

When we got to the top of the hill my friend said, "He is not going to stop. Let go."

And off he went. It scared me so bad that I lost my grip and off I went. My friend landed on his stomach and skidded down the road. It tore his coat up pretty good, wearing out the brass buttons. Me, I was not so lucky. I started rolling on the edge of the road, there was a break in the concrete pavement, and my head hit it, knocking several holes in my head. One of the older boys was sitting on the front porch and witnessed the incident. He noticed a large 18-wheeler bearing down on me, and he ran in front of the truck and snatched me out of the path of the truck. He saved my life from the fall and after several days in the hospital I was shooting marbles and playing cowboys again. The boy that saved me told Mom and Dad he didn't know where the burst of speed came from but God must have taken charge. I don't ever remember riding on the rear bumper of a pickup truck again.

The houses built back then were well off the ground and us kids would play under them. We would use a brick to make roads and half pint bottles for our cars. The way Highway 74 was there was a high bank above the ditch almost 12 feet high and lots of times we would just go over to the bank and sit and watch vehicles go by. Not many vehicles were on the roads back then.

One hot summer day we were sitting on the bank and this elderly woman who was blind came down the road with her guide dog. She would do this several times a week for exercise I guess, but we would always speak to her and soon she could tell who was there by our voices. We liked the lady and her dog and would never do anything to hurt her or the dog. Well, this man who lived on Mill Hill came by and later he told Dad that I was throwing rocks at the woman and dog. When I came home dad was waiting for me with a razor strap. I didn't know why he beat me until after he got tired. Then he told me that Wilbur had told him that I was throwing rocks at the lady and her dog. I tried to tell him it was not so, but he wouldn't believe me. Wilbur was nothing but a drunk anyway, but I have never forgiven him for what he did.

The first really good Christmas gift I ever received was at Ida Mill. Dad bought me a bicycle and I was so excited about it. Instead of pushing it off the porch and down the steps, I rode it, lost control, and ran into the side of the neighbor's house bending the front wheel so badly that I couldn't ride it until dad bought a new wheel. Another thing I remember was that Brooks had a dog and every once in a while the old dog would have a fit and would be foaming at the mouth and we would run from the dog as he would try to catch us but in his condition he couldn't run just wobble around.

I remember once we were playing with other kids and this one girl had long hair. She was in the chicken fence at her home and for some reason, I don't remember, I pulled her hair through the chicken wire and tied it in a knot and I left her there. When we all got Red Ryder BB guns, we used to play cowboys and shoot at each other. Several times one of the kids would get hurt, but the old things wouldn't go over 15 yards at an arch.

I remember one Sunday Dad, Pete, and some of the others had gone to Whiteville to see Grandpa Ikner and Mom stayed home with us kids. After dinner, most of the women dipped their snuff and Mom took us down the street to Mrs. Meekins. She was sitting on the front porch so she could spit her snuff in the front yard.

After awhile I noticed two of the neighbor's children go around the side of our house with a bucket. I figured they were up to no good so I asked Mom if I could go back to the house and she said ok, but not to get into any trouble. Well, trouble I found. When I went around the side of the house, they had a bucket full of our coal. I told them to put the coal back or I would get them. That was a mistake I made. The girl reached down, picked up a large piece of coal just before I got to her and she hit me on the side of the head by my temple, knocking a large hole in my head. They ran and left the bucket full of coal sitting there but mom heard me cry out and came running back home. She sent Annette off looking for someone with a car to take me to the hospital, while she tried to stop the bleeding. By the time they had got me to the hospital I had lost so much blood that I was almost in shock. I remained in the hospital for several days until I was strong enough to go home. I learned a lesson. Never threaten someone who is standing in a coal pile.

While at Ida Mill, I was small, and got picked on a lot but the most was by Doris, a girl. She didn't like me because I was afraid of her and a many of times I had to do some hard running to get away from her. When Robert (man) was with me she never would pick on me because she was afraid of Robert and what he would do to her. Her whole family was something else. Once her dad got mad with one of his mules and he shot it in the field, dug a hole and buried it right where it laid.

Her brother was killed and placed on the railroad for the train to hit him. Once, Dad said a man came home and caught him with his wife and he cut him from one cheek to the other and threw him down the hill in the ditch to bleed to death, but Dad saw him lying side the road when they were coming in from work and carried him to the hospital. Dad said it took over 200 stitches to sew his tail back on. Not long after that is when he was hit by that train.

In the winter months were hog killing time and I remember we had a hog named Billy. Billy was so large they had to drag it to the house with a truck and the 55-gallon drum was too small to get him in so they had to hang him from a large tree to bleed him and scrape him by pouring hot water on him. Everyone around would pitch in at killing time and sometimes 10-15 hogs would be killed in one weekend. The weather had to be cold also.

I remember at this one killing that Walter and Betty were helping and most times the man would share the meat with others, especially the parts that they didn't want. Well, that day was the first time I had ever met Betty's mom and dad. They came up the drive in an old car and I remember saying there come some blacks to get some meat and Walter told me it was Betty's mom and dad, not to call them blacks.

Later I found out she was Indian. It's funny how little bits will stay with you a long time.

When we played cowboys, I always wanted to be Sunset Carson because he rode a white horse and carried two guns. I remember about the graveyard. The story was told that a young woman had died and her parents had put up a Cedar tree near the front of her grave and someone stole it and often she would appear looking for the tree. I have thought I saw someone on several occasions, because it got to where when I would walk on the road I would start running and run for several hundred yards. I was afraid, especially if I was alone.

I also remember the time we were down at the pond and you could jump off the dam and make it to the sandbar and then you could walk out of the pond. Well, I had not learned how to swim and that day we had been playing for a long time, and I guess I was tired. I dived in and I missed the sandbar and the water was 10-12 feet deep. I was hollering for help and I guess everyone thought I was playing and finally Barbara Lewis saw that I was in trouble and she dove in and pulled me to safety. I don't remember how many times I had gone down but I know I had taken in a lot of water. But thanks to her, she saved me that day.

I also remember the day Mom and Dad came to the schoolhouse and I and several other boys were being punished for double riding the swings and causing the frame to turn over. I was standing at the chalkboard with my nose in a circle and we had to stay that way without taking our noses out of the small circles until the teacher told us to take our seats. If your nose left the blackboard, it would leave a print and when the teacher checked then she could tell and would make us stay longer. Well, that day Mom and Dad went to the schoolhouse because they were taking pictures and they went to have their pictures taken with Annette and they saw me being punished.

Every Christmas we would know what we were going to get because the house only had one small closet. Getting a nickel to buy candy was a real treat. They built a drive-in movie and some nights we would go there and get on the back row where we wouldn't be seen and see the movie.

The old cotton gin was operating at that time also. I remember once going in the gin and the men caught us and threw us in the cotton baler but they stopped it before it got to the presser. I never went in there again.

When the news came out that World War II had ended some of us went to the church, we would always unlock some windows in case we wanted to get in, and started ringing the church bell for a long time. Walter and Junior had both served early in the war. Walter was a Paratrooper and Junior was in the Navy. Junior got wounded, and a plate had to be put in the back of his head. He acted a little crazy after that.

We went back to Whiteville once more with Mr. Butler, the same house we had lived in before but we didn't stay there long, just until tobacco season was over. I remember Dad bought a gas lamp and the old house lit up so bright that the neighbors thought it had caught on fire and came over to help put it out.

Dad would buy ice cream and cones and we would get treated about every time he went to get groceries. I remember staring at New Hope School again because, me, Rosa Lee, and Shotgun all got the chicken pox at the same time and after that Dad bought the house on South Main Street in Laurinburg. That house had four rooms and a bath and also a large garage in the back. I remember Dad fixing the garage up and Flora Bell stayed in it for a while. We went to Central School and lived in the city limits.

The bus would not pick us up so we had to walk to school. There were lots of kids in the neighborhood and we had lots of good times. We had ourselves a club called, "The Captain Kidd Club." With our own identifying marks we drew on our hands. We made us a small camp area down in the woods and we played a lot there. I was a very good marble shooter. I had broken my right thumb and never went to the doctor and it grew back straight, that gave me extra strength. We played a lot of baseball and football, but I didn't like basketball. Comics were also something we did. I sure did read a lot of them and later on when we had to do book reports in school I would buy the ones about history and do my reports on them. I know the teacher never thought they were comics.

When I started to school at Laurinburg High School, I would get 25 cents a day for lunch. We were not supposed to leave the school grounds but we did anyway and would go to *Pete Jones' Trading Post* to eat. He would fix hamburgers and hot dogs for us kids, and they were 10 cents each and five cents for a drink. He would give you a ticket with each hot dog or hamburger and at Christmas and the end of school he would have a drawing and give away prizes. One year at Christmas, I won the bike and boy was I proud. I remember Santa getting me a model airplane, the kind that ran and had control wires. Well, I was going over to the American Legion area to fly my new plane and I didn't pay attention to traffic crossing the road. I looked up and an 18-wheeler was headed straight for me and I tried to hurry across the road, losing my balance on the bike and falling to the road. I grabbed the plane but I couldn't save the bike. The truck hit it and tore it all to pieces. Trying to fly the plane, I crashed it and tore it beyond repair also.

In the summer months between school, I would go to Grandpa and Grandma Rasberry's and help them on the farm. It was always hard work but I enjoyed being with Granddad, and I knew he needed all the help he could get. The first year I remembered was when he lived on the Cox's farm between Whiteville and Chadbourn on Old Highway 74. I don't remember much except when all our chores were done for the day we would sit on the front porch and watch cars passing by and hoping someday to have one of our own. The old green wooden rocking chairs sure did stand the taste of time because when she passed away she still had one on their front porch. I remember Flora Bell, SM, and Shelby and the times when we would get some candy or a drink from the store, now that was a real treat.

I think the following year Granddad moved a mile or so east toward Whiteville but closer to the little country store. I don't have any remembrance of that place. I know the older I got the more chores I got - plowing fields by myself and driving the mules at tobacco time. I never did help with the corn because I would have to go back to school before it was ready. Granddad always planted field peas in the cornrow middles so we would have late peas. He also had plenty of watermelons and cantaloupes for us to eat. Chickens were our Sunday meal, but usually it was the roosters we got because the hens were used to produce the eggs and the baby chickens.

The next place I remember was behind the *Columbus County Country Club* off Highway 710 between Whiteville and Clarkton. It was a very nice place and the neighbors were very kind to us. They would give us all the milk we wanted to drink and sometimes when he needed extra help he would pay us a little money to help out. He had a daughter I was sweet on, I don't even remember her name, but I was very young and very bashful.

I remember all the times plowing in the fields from sun up to sun down and would be so tired at night you wouldn't even remember going to bed. We had to wash in a barrel so at noon when you came in to eat you would have to draw the water from the well and fill your barrel so the sun could heat it. We still had an outhouse. Our icebox was a hole under the house with feed sacks in them to help keep the ice from melting so fast. The iceman usually came by twice a week and he'd also sold candy. So every now and then we would get a treat. Our week's work was usually finished at noon Saturday so we had 11/2 days to rest up for the next week. Being skilled workers we would fashion us golf clubs out of tree limbs and put some shoe heel taps on them and time to time just before dark and all the golfers were gone we would go over to the pond on the course, pull off our clothes and swim for awhile and find golf balls in the water and we would play our own version of golf. It was our way of finishing off a hard day's work.

I remember one Saturday in particular, it had been reported on the battery-powered radio (still no electricity) that a circus had been in Whiteville and that one of the panthers had escaped and they had not found it, so please be careful because it was very dangerous. Well, Grandma wanted something from the store, about a mile from the house, and she told Shelby she could go. That made me and SM mad because we knew she would get some candy and we wouldn't. There was a lot of woods on the left side of the road going to the store and almost 200 yards on the right side we would climb in the trees at times when we were playing in the area to see further down the road.

Well, after Shelby left to go to the store, SM and I said we were going to the golf course to hit some balls. It was getting toward sundown when we saw Shelby coming back. We had gotten up in one of the trees. We could hear her singing and really enjoying herself, and as she got near us I let out a loud squall, like a large cat, Shelby stopped in her tracks, screamed, and fainted dead cold. I guess the thought of a panther being on the loose, the long cry, and the trees shaking, just about scared her to death. It surely did scare SM and I. She finally came to and when we got her to the house the first thing she did was tell Grandma, and I thought we were really going to get a beating, but we were spared. Shelby can tell the story a lot better than I can.

I remember one evening Grandma sent me to get 2 gallons of milk from the neighbor. We had a shortcut path through the woods to the road so the trip would be shorter because two gallon jars of milk gets heavy. Well, this evening Grandma was sitting in the front yard grading tobacco and it was about sunset when I was coming back home, and as I was coming down the path I stopped dead in my tracks. A very large snake, the biggest I had ever seen, like the ones Tarzan fought in his movies, was crossing the path and I could feel it pushing against the end of my toes. It seemed like it took ten minutes to cross the path.

After it passed, I started running as hard as I could toward the house and when I got into the yard I hollered for Grandma and it scared her and she threw the tobacco in her lap in the air and the chair she was sitting in fell over backwards and she started hollering also. We laughed about it later and Granddad went out looking for this monstrous snake I had seen but he couldn't find it. It got too dark.

One summer when I had stayed with Grandpa and Grandma. Dad had bought me a motorbike but I could never get it to start except on Sundays so I traded it for a single shot .22 Cal rifle (I still have it). That must have been in 1949. Well, I took it with me that summer. I would take it to the tobacco barns when we would have to cure the tobacco. Someone would have to be awake at all times to keep the fire going and the inside temperature right. It would make us feel protected to have it with us.

I remember me and Granddad had gone out early one morning to cut pine trees for the next curing of tobacco and I took the rifle with me. I told Grandpa it was to shoot snakes if we say any. It was almost dark when we started back to the house and I saw a large crow circling in the sky.

I said to Grandpa, "Do you think I can hit the bird?"

And I remember him laughing and say, "No way could you hit that bird."

I didn't even aim the rifle. I just pointed it up toward the circling bird and pulled the trigger. Bingo. The bird fell. Granddad couldn't believe it and told me the bird must have had a heart attack when he heard the shot. We searched for the bird until we found it and sure enough the bullet went through its body. The rest of summer they called me, "Dead Eye Billy."

I loved my grandparents very much and it hurt me to see Granddad rolling his cigarettes out of the cheapest tobacco he could buy or twisting leaves to dry out when curing and he would cut them up fine and smoke them. Sometimes he would cough from one cigarette to the next. I knew one day it would tell on him. Well, those were fun filled summers for me, a lot of hard work and a valuable lesson learned in helping those in need. I know there is a lot more but time has erased my memory pretty good.

I remember when I was smaller, before I started going to Grandpa Rasberry's, the 4th of July was a time to go to Grandpa

Ikner's for the big celebration. Most all the Ikner kids would pack up their families and head to Whiteville. On Saturday, the men would go squirrel hunting to get our Sunday dinner. Now, you are talking about 75 - 100 folks to feed. They would skin those little things and they would be cooked all kinds of ways, fried, boiled with rice, and diced up to season collards or cabbage. There would be lots of pork and beef and sweet potatoes for every one. For Sunday I'll bet there were 200 biscuits cooked and cakes and pies everywhere. It would be a great dinner with folks eating everywhere, log lunches, porches, steps and on the ground.

They would always have fireworks until one year they had some large firecrackers and Walter was setting them off, one didn't go off and he told me to get it and bring it back to him. Just as I picked it up, being a kid and not knowing the danger, it went off in my hand and like to have blew my thumb off my right hand. No more fireworks.

One story I liked to have left out was when we lived in Ida Mill. I was helping Rosa Lee clear out a spot where she could make a playhouse, using the sharp hoe to chop the weeds and my toe on my right foot got in the way and I almost cut it off. Mom put iodine on it and taped it real tight and it healed back. Now in very cold weather that toe will almost freeze and ache like crazy.

Uncle Rue bought me a bicycle. A fancy *Shelby* bike, black with a horn, light and action on the front wheel. Boy it was something. He didn't just give it to me. I got a job delivering the *Raleigh News and Observer*, an afternoon paper, and I used the bike on the paper route. I would have to make weekly payments on the bike. 50 cents. It went well for a while, but the weight of the newspapers and the long route took its toll on the bike, new chains, tires, etc. and finally Dad said he couldn't afford for me to keep delivering papers so I had to stop.

Then, I got a job working as a clerk at *Anthony's Grocery* on Main Street in Laurinburg. I worked Monday evenings from school out to 9 pm. It was taking a toll on my homework. My grades were going down. I continued to work for Mr. Anthony except the summer months when I was packed up and sent to Grandpa's. When I got 15 years old they let me work part time in the mill. With *Anthony's*, I worked Mondays, Fridays, and all day Saturday and I got $7.50, a lot of money at that time for a boy. But the cotton mill, I got 75 cent an hour sweeping floors, so I made more money. I did this in the evenings after school from five to eight p.m.

I loved to play baseball and football but working all the time and low grades, they wouldn't let me on the high school team but I did play softball with the FFA (Future Farmers of America) team because that was during school time. I also ran track with them. I was small but I could run like a deer. When the 10th grade was over, I turned sixteen and I could work 8 hours a day in the Mill, big money.

Pat Burroughs was my neighbor and friend and we got the silly idea of getting our parents to sign for us to get in the Navy. I remember going with Pat Jr. to Raeford, NC to get his birth certificate and he had bought a car from Pete Easterling and on the way back from Raeford, about three miles from home it caught on fire and we left it burning on the side of the road, 401 north of Laurinburg. When we got home, Pat and I went to Mr. Easterling and Pat Jr. told him his car was on the road north of Laurinburg. Boy, was he mad.

Well, back to the Navy. We tried to change our birth certificates to make us a year older than we really were and Dad and Mrs. Burroughs went to Lumberton to sign for us. Well, it went good that day and we were told to go home and we would be hearing from them in about ten days. We did. I guess they saw how we changed our birth certificates and sent us a letter telling us our true age.

When school started back I talked Mom and Dad into letting me work instead of going back to school. I had failed 10th grade English, and I knew it would be hard. They finally agreed it would be better for me to work than force me to school to fail. I guess I thought I was grown then, and I started slipping around and drinking beer at

Southern Junction, which was run by Uncle Rue and Aunt Janie Mae. It didn't take but a couple for me to get tipsy.

The first car I had was in a partnership with Pat Jr. and Bill Elmore and myself. We bought an A-Model Coupe with a rumble back seat together for $25.00. It wouldn't start with the starter so every time we cranked it we had to push it. I don't remember what ever happened to it.

The next one I had was a '35 Chevy Sedan, 4 seater. I didn't like the color so we painted it red, white, and blue. Boy did it stand out. I didn't have my driver's license when I got it, so if I went anywhere, H.C. Herring or Richard Deaton would drive it. I remember one day Richard was driving, and we got in a wreck at the corner of Biggs and Vance Street. There wasn't a stop sign and a neighbor driver stopped and we ran together, causing only minor damage. I remember the police came to the scene, and he didn't charge either driver and told us to be careful at intersections.

I guess I had the car for about 10 months. I left it in the bottom of a river somewhere in South Carolina. The bridge was out and there were no warnings, plus we had been drinking beer, and I guess I was driving too fast, but the car sank to the bottom, but we were able to get out unharmed except shaken up a bit and in the middle of nowhere.

I was sweet on a girl back then, Sylvia Cole, who lived on 6th street in East Laurinburg. I met Betty Lou on a double date, she was going with Pat Jr. in September of 1951. This is about the time I first heard of Betty Lou Moody. She was seeing my friend, Pat Burroughs, and he would tell me about his going out to see her.

Dad put me on the second shift with Carson McKinsey working the *Barbara Coleman Warper*. I guess that way he figured he would keep me out of trouble. It worked, too. He would work me six days a week from 3:30 - 11:30 P.M. and on Saturday nights I would have to clean up. Sunday was the only day I had off and most of the time I wanted to just rest up. I always did have a little crush on Doris Goodwin. She lived down the street and Pat Ellis, too, and there was the cook girl, Evelyn, on the corner. So, I liked a lot of girls. Well, enough of that.

In June 1952, I was turning 17 years old and the Korean War was in full swing, and I really wanted to go. Dad signed for me to get in the Army and I was sworn in June 24, 1952 in Charlotte, NC. After a couple of days orientation in Charlotte, they shipped a lot of us to Ft. Jackson S.C. I was in H Co 28th Inf Reg for my basic training. Before I went in I thought I was tough and the first two weeks I found out what tough was. After my first meal at Fort Jackson's Consolidated Mess hall, I spent 24 hours peeling potatoes for throwing a piece of half-done chicken in the garbage can. That was my first lesson learned. Whatever they gave you to eat, eat it or put it in your helmet and take it away from the mess hall.

Billy in his uniform

Basic training was 16 weeks of very demanding training and at Ft. Jackson that summer, it was the hottest I have ever encountered.

Heavy clothing/heavy packs/belt equipment and a rifle that topped that off. I never did like wearing hats and that steel helmet kept my neck and shoulders sore. There weren't any trucks to take you from training area to training area and boy did we have to run a lot to make it on time. There was no excuse for being late for training. After a hard day of training, at night work never stopped. There was K.P. (Kitchen Police), Guard duty, Fire Guard (Firing the wooden boilers so we would have hot water). On top of that you had to hand wash the clothes you wore that day and press them under your mattress at night, clean your weapons, and the barracks had to be cleaned by 9:30 P.M. for inspection. Lights out at 10 P.M., 11 P.M. on Saturday night.

I had a hard time memorizing things so I never got a pass on the weekend because they would ask you questions when you went to get the 12 hour pass (12 P.M. - 12 A.M. Saturday). I would study hard in one area and they would ask questions on something else. Oh, well. I didn't waste any money downtown.

Mom and Dad and all came several times while I was in training. Certain weekends if we performed well during the week they would let you have visitors on Saturday evening or Sunday after church. We had to attend church if we were not on some kind of work detail.

At the service club on post on Saturday night they would usually put on shows and we could go watch them. A lot of the country stars were stationed at Fort Jackson. They would put on some good shows, picking and singing. Sometimes the crowds were so large they would go to the football stadium to put on the shows. I know before I joined the army I liked Elizabeth Denson from Maxton and she visited once with Mom and Dad.

When training at Fort Jackson was over I had passed the physical to go to jump school training at Fort Benning, GA. I wanted to be a Paratrooper. I thought basic training was rough, well let me tell you, jump school either made you or broke you.

We didn't get a break from Basic. We graduated on Friday evening and were on buses Saturday morning to Fort Benning, GA. I remember when we got there after riding the buses for almost seven hours they took us to *Simmons Airfield*, unloaded us, put us in formation, grounded our duffle bags and ran us 5 miles, got our heavy duffle bags and marched us 2 and a half miles to the barracks we would be staying at. I don't think they even fed us that night because at 9 P.M. lights out, up at 11:30 P.M. out for physical training to 5:30 A.M., back in the barracks, shower, shave, and back in formation at 5:55 A.M., return at 6:00 A.M., breakfast, back to the barracks for inspection at 7:00 A.M., training formation at 7:15 A.M. You think that won't wake you up, well, it will. I must have run 500 miles and done 20,000 push-ups before the four weeks of training.

We had a Christmas break, and then back for the final week, when we did all the Airborne jumps (five jumps) Tuesday - Thursday, Graduation on Friday and ship out on Saturday. Boy what a week. I got back early off Christmas break and a bunch of us decided to go to Columbus on Saturday night. I should have stayed on base, because I drank a couple of beers and the saying was you couldn't graduate unless you got the insignia from one of the Engineers on post. After a couple of beers I could take on the whole foreigner Battalion by myself.

Later on that night, I had my chance and all of us landed in jail and the company First Sergeant had to come to town to get us out. I lost my hat during the fight and I had to wire Mom and Dad because the MP's took what money I had left in my pocketbook and said I didn't have any, to send me some money so I could get a hat before Friday's graduation. I was already in hot water with the First Sergeant because I was on Fire Guard one night, and I was supposed to be relieved at 1 A.M. and the guy never showed up and later on I fell asleep and the boilers went out in all the barracks. They made me pull K.P. the next night and the guy who didn't relieve me, they didn't do anything to him. It sure did make me mad and the Mess Sergeant knew I was mad and he wouldn't let me in the cooking area. He was afraid I might screw up the supper meal, so he put me in the grease traps cleaning them, the worst job on K.P.

Finally, I got my wings and boy was I a proud soldier.

Billy Ikner, Airborne

I was sent to Fort Bragg with the 505th Airborne Infantry Regiment, HG and HG company. The 505 was an all black regiment at one time and after they broke it up there were a lot of black sergeants left in the regiment. My Platoon Sergeant was one and I always did what I was told to do. The Regiment was in Watertown, NY for winter training, so after a couple of days of orientation, we were issued our cold winter gear, loaded on 2 1/2 ton trucks and trucked to New York. It took us two days to get there about the 10th of January, 1953, I arrived in New York. Boy was it cold. I wasn't used to ice and snow but at Camp Drum, it was frozen.

We had to learn how to ski, which I never could. I couldn't even skate much less ski on ice, but I sure did have to try. We made one training jump in the snow and it was great. The experience was about to close out and we were supposed to jump in and we had to fight (simulate) our way back to Camp Drum and we would then load the rest of our equipment and head back to Fort Bragg. (Before this, we made another jump and the drop zone had frozen over and it was a disaster. Lots of injuries). Well, we didn't get to make the final jump because of the weather so they made us jump from the back of moving 2 1/2 ton trucks. I remember it was getting late in the evening. It got dark early up there when we finally got all our company together. They had issued us enough C-Rations for 2 days and the last day we would be heading back into Camp Drum. My Platoon SGT. sent me out with another soldier who had a 3.5 rocket launcher to guard the flank position while we were in the assembly area. He told us to leave our packs and we could get them when we came back in, that he would send after us. Well, we waited and waited and no one came after us and it was so dark you couldn't see five feet in front of you.

I told the guy, "Man, let's go back and find out what's going on."

Well, would you believe we could not find anyone or hear anything? Man that had me in a panic. We had our little flashlights but you had to use the red lens and as dark as it was it didn't do any good. Told him we had better take off back South. We walked and walked, we hadn't eaten since breakfast, was cold, lost, and really didn't know where to go. It seemed like we had been walking for about five hours and I spotted a fire in the distance. I set my sights on it. It took us about another hour to get to it walking in the heavy ice and patches of snow.

When we got to the fire, it was an aggressor's ammunition dump and the guys were burning ammunition boxes to help keep warm. They let us stay by the fire but they would take us as prisoners. They did share some C-Rations with us. We melted snow in our helmets and refilled our canteens with water. It was daylight before I got to sleep, I think, and the guys told us we had to leave their area before judges came by and pointed us in the direction of Camp Drum.

We never did get up with our outfit but we made it back to Camp Drum well before the company did. In fact, we were there a day before they got in. The Platoon SGT. was very angry and said we had deserted from our post. I told the Company Commander what happened and he reprimanded the SGT. for what he did. We could have gotten lost, froze to death, hurt, who knows? I know the Platoon SGT. hated me for going to the Company Commander.

We were not back at Ft. Bragg long before we were sent off again, this time to the desert outside of Las Vegas, Nevada on what was called Exercise Knot Hole but the Air Force. The place we went to was Desert Rock, a Nuclear Test area and it was in the middle of nowhere. I remember riding the troop train out there and playing poker and winning over $500.00. I had me some money when we arrived. One morning we stopped in Kansas City, MO. to pick up food cars and it was about 3 A.M. They got us up and we went for a long run, singing our Airborne songs all over the area by the train station.

I remember stopping once to pick up cars and it was way out in the country but you could see a store about a half mile away and all of a sudden about 20 kids came riding out on horseback. The GIs were giving the kids money to go get them drinks and stuff from the store. After the kids got the money, we never saw them again.

Desert Rock was nothing but a bunch of squad size tents set up with folding banks on dirt floors. A large tent for the beer hall and shower tents. Boy, it was hot and we did several days training and lots of physical training and getting us to wear our gas mask for long periods of time. If you could come up with $20.00 in cash, they would let you go into Las Vegas on Saturday and return in the P.M. I was able to go once and all I did was lose most of my money gambling and eating.

We did a dry run of what we were supposed to do on D-day as they called it. They carried us out to an area about an hour by bus from Desert Rock and there they had long trenches dug. We could also see the very tall tower set up in a mock town a couple of thousand yards away. They put us in the trenches and people came by and were telling us what to do when the explosion went off. Brace ourselves in the trenches until after the shock wave passed, not to look up until we were told to exit the trenches and we walked down to the village or town they had set up. They loaded us back up and we went back to Desert Rock.

The beer tent had all the free beer you wanted to drink and some of the guys stayed high a lot. I knew we were going to have to do a lot of physical training so I stayed away from it. It was hot, dusty during the daytime and cold at night. Finally, D-Day came. Back to the trenches. At one time rumors was that they were going to drop the bomb and we were going to parachute in behind it. So, we were all probably a little tense and we saw the trenches and then we knew that was not going to happen. They told us it was nothing to worry about and chemical people would be monitoring us throughout the exercise.

I know we didn't have any idea of what we were about to witness. I never did see where the control bunkers were and didn't really care. We were able to hear the countdown to the explosion, you heard it and as the shock wave passed over the heat was right behind it. I know I looked up and I saw this huge fireball going up in the sky. We were told to exit the trenches and we started walking toward ground zero and later were told as we got closer to put on the gas mask. I didn't think you could burn a cactus, but I saw them burning.

The mock town was totally destroyed. They had set out old vehicles. They were thrown everywhere and the tiers and canvases were burning. And the huge mushroom cloud just kept rising in the sky. I don't how long we were exposed to the fallout but I would guess 2 - 3 hours. I know when we got to ground zero, sheep, goats, chickens, and I don't know what all were burned to a crisp. The smell of the burning flesh was terrible. We had to remove our mask as we approached ground zero - we were taken back to the buses, swept off with a broom, body checked with a Geiger Counter IM 94 or something like that and returned to base camp where we had to shower and put on clean clothing. The whole trip was about three weeks if I remember correctly. Then it was back to Fort Bragg on a troop train.

Back at Ft. Bragg, it was training as usual. The first night jump we made after returning to Bragg. I remember the jump commander was a little nervous about jumping because the winds had picked up somewhat, but everyone was ready to get it over with, so up we went.

By the time we left, the winds were over 35 miles per hour and boy did we have problems. Somehow or another myself and another jumper became entangled before we hit the ground and I had no control over my parachute. Plus I was swinging back and forth, not side to side to make a safe PLF. Sometimes during the descent I got cords entangled around my neck and I also landed on a large stump that was still laying on the drop zone. I woke up in the hospital with my back and neck in terrible pain. When the doctor came in, he told me I was very lucky to be alive. I had cuts on my throat and a broken back.

Well, it took several months in the hospital and in the barracks before I went back to duty, which was light duty. My new job was cleaning up officer's quarters. It was not a demeaning job because you could pick up extra money shining shoes, which I was very good at. I only had to report to my Platoon SGT. once a month at Post Muster. I liked that also. Everything was going good for me until the Platoon SGT. had to get back into it with me. One day I was not feeling good and he started harassing me and I finally lost it. I hit him across the head with my entracking tool (shovel) several times.

I grabbed some clothes in my bag and took off. I wound up in Richmond, VA with my Aunt Louise. Well, the Army got in touch with Dad and he and Mom finally found where I was and they came and got me and carried me back to Ft. Bragg. That was the worst thing I could have done at the time - going AWOL, because the next thing I knew I was on orders to go to Japan with the 187th Airborne Regt. in Bipor, Japan. I got over there in November and the post was very small in a walled in area with barbed wire on top, two gates moved by the MP's. Basically, all we did was train, PT, and jump. To get a pass to town you had to earn that pass. I guess the whole time I was there late February 1954, I only went to town maybe six times. I met J.C. Fore over there. He was from Laurinburg and had married a Japanese woman. I visited his home once. They had one child.

I was not able to continue jumping because the pressure was too much on my back when I tried to put on the parachute. There were about 14 of us not on jump stations so they sent us to Korea with the 25th Infantry Division. I thought that it was cold in Japan, but I liked to have froze in Korea.

They loaded us up on a train with wooden seats, half of the

windows gone, and cold fired. It took us about fourteen hours to get to the 25th Division Headquarters. Cold, hungry, and it was snowing when we arrived. They fed us, gave us a sleeping bag and told us to get some sleep. It seemed like I had just closed my eyes when they came around telling us to get up, shave and get ready for chow. After chow, we were given a series of shots, issued winter clothing, weapons, and by 11 A.M., we were on trucks heading to our new unit.

I was sent to H. Company 27th Infantry Wolfhounds at Camp Hovey. Camp Hovey was a tent city, muddy in the rainy season, hot and dusty in the hot days. We got to shower and change clothes every three days. There was only one shower tent for the whole regiment. We were responsible for rebuilding the Kansas Line. I think I must have filled a million sand bags rebuilding bunkers. I know we went on a field exercise and after a couple of weeks water was hard to keep and boy was it hot and humid and one day they sent three of us with canteens to look for a water well. We found some but the iodine tablets didn't work and I got very sick and hot to be sent back into the hospital. Well, you wouldn't believe it but while I was in the hospital, they decided that I needed to be circumcised and did they butchered me but good.

After I got out of the hospital, I was sent to I Corp NCO Academy. I didn't do too bad. I was 34th out of 100 cadets. After I got back to my unit in July, I was promoted to Corporal. And in September, I was promoted to Sergeant. So, it pays off for me to go to the academy. Well, the 25th was preparing to go back to Hawaii. I was picked to go back from my regiment on an advance party to help set up a NCO Academy to train leaders who would be coming back with the main party. It was some trip back. You had to load on large Navy ships from smaller ones and I was made SGT. of the Guard on the ship. I didn't have to do much, because there was a storm and we had to stay below deck most of the way back.

We really had our job cut out for us because the old wooden barracks we were given to start the NCO Academy were in a poor state of repair, they still had bullet holes in them from WWII. We worked hard and when the main party arrived we were ready. In January 1955 we started the 1st class at the Academy. That was the first time I had ever got up and gave classes and for the first time I did really good. I did this until June 1955, then I rotated back to Ft. Benning, GA. I was assigned to Conare Board #3, test unit.

That summer while on leave, I met the love of my life for the second time. Betty was like a magnet for me. I couldn't stay away from her. I hated to go to Ft. Benning, but I wrote her every chance I got. Ft. Banning was another new experience for me, but I caught on really fast and I was assigned to test a weapon soon after I got there, the Claymore Mine. I sure did miss Betty and I thought of her all the time. I guess it was sometime in August I wrote Betty a letter and told her I would be home for the weekend of Labor Day and to be ready and we would get married on Saturday night and I would have to go back to Ft. Benning on Monday evening to go to work on Tuesday morning.

We had a beautiful wedding in Bennettsville, SC and the poor car we were in everyone was packed like sardines. We spent our first night together at Pete and Tiny's house and the 2nd night at Howard and Millie's house. Betty was a beautiful bride and she still is 45 years later. She told me she didn't know what her mother would say when she told her but Myrtle knew I was the only one for Betty.

I left after dinner on Monday and I drove 9 hours and was in a cloud, a love cloud. I guess I wrote Betty every night and I had to start looking for us a place to live that we could afford on my salary. I found a small, small trailer with the rent only $50.00 per month and I started buying little things that we would need to set up housekeeping. One of Betty's friends had a shower for her so we got some things there. We still have the set of pots I bought at Sears, pink handles, and we have them now. When Betty came down, Mom, Dad, Annette, Myrtle, and Danny came also and we had to sleep some of them with the neighbors, but we made out.

Billy and Betty, Georgia, 1955 (right after marriage)

It was a hard go for us but we loved each other and was determined to make it work and it did. A penny saved was spent on a time need before the next payday. We still have our first Christmas tree but I don't remember what we gave each other for Christmas. I had a 1950 Ford Convertible and the top was messed up so when we got our 1st income tax check we had a new top put on the car in Laurinburg and I took what was left and bought Betty an ironing board and we still use it today. But the car is long gone.

Betty

The first television we got was a 17 inch and we bought it with a little down and a little a month and they gave us an am clock radio free. We still have it and it still plays. I remember Betty gave me a birthday dinner for my 21st birthday and some of the neighbors came. Betty was pregnant with Ricky. We knew the trailer was too small when the baby came, so I started looking for something larger. We found a two-bedroom apartment that we could afford for a while anyways. After Ricky was born, I found a cheap place to stay with enough room for the three of us, a garage turned into an apartment. We stayed there until I got orders for Korea in 1958. Betty moved back to Laurinburg and stayed with Mom and Dad for the 13 months I was in Korea.

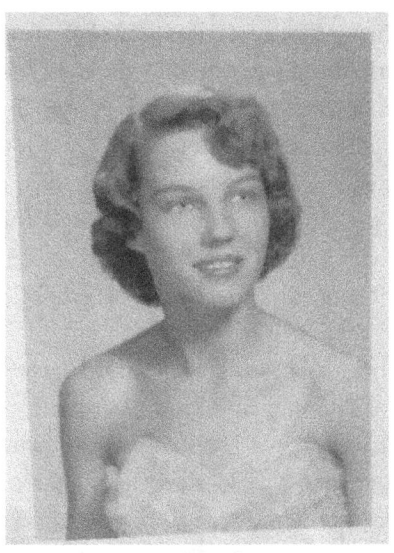
Betty, 1958, Age 18

When I came back I was stationed in the same unit I left from so it was back to Ft. Benning. We found a house this time, 2 bedrooms in a nice neighborhood. We stayed there for awhile and I was able to get one a lot cheaper and closer to the post so we moved again. We stayed there until we left for Hawaii in 1962. While at Ft. Benning, I loved to play sports and I was on the company's fast pitch softball team, Left Fielders, and I also played on the flag football team. Betty and Ricky would always go to the games.

It was during my first tour that an incident happened in my life. I was a test NCO and we were running tests one day and I had CQ duty that night and we were running late so the Col. asked if one of the SGTs. could fill in for my duty and I could take theirs when it came up and another SGT. said he would. Well, that night the company mail clerk went berserk and shot one round from a 22 Cal. pistol and hit the SGT. and killed him. His life ended because he took my place on duty. That was a real pain for me. Again, my life had been spared.

About the only other event was I broke a finger horse playing and broke my wrist playing football. We went to Hawaii in June 1962 and I was stationed with the 1st Brigade, 25th Infantry Division (Garden Dragons). I had quit smoking in 1960 but I still drank beer. I was put into the nuclear weapons platoon and it being new we had to train the three teams. I had tested the Davy Crockett system at Ft. Benning so I was the expert in the field. I started drinking more than usual and I still was a SGT. and promotions never did come on the 25th.

Every three months my platoon would have to go to the big Island for Support Training of one of the battalions and they lasted about 21 days. The first time I went over I got sick one Saturday at the NCO Club and on Sunday morning we started a three day fold exercise and I blamed my sickness on the beers I had drank on Saturday evening and that was the last beer I have ever drank and that was in January 1963. It was a wonderful experience to be in Hawaii, but on SGT. pay we knew we didn't have any money to spend extra so we did our own entertainment by going to free shows at the bases and hamburger/hotdog cookouts at the beaches with friends.

John and Patty Dunham, Bob and Liz Kin, and us became good friends. I remember us playing cards on the weekends all night some time. I remember the time we took Ricky to KoaKola pass (where the Japanese attacked to start World War II) and he got away from me and liked to have run off the cliff. Scared me to death almost. Betty missed seeing her family a lot but we had each other that made it a lot easier. David and Candy were over there also and Jeanette and Ed Carpenter.

Billy Ikner in uniform

The three years went by pretty fast and it was back on the boat heading for Ft. Jackson, SC, my new assignment. After a few days leave, we decided to check out Ft. Jackson and when personnel found out I was Airborne qualified I was cut new orders and sent to Ft. Bragg, NC. We decided to buy a house in Laurinburg and I drove to Ft. Bragg. So, we found a nice house at that time that we could afford and we settled in on Morgan Circle. I was assigned to 82nd Administrative Company as operating SGT. Everything was going fine and finally I was promoted to SSG E6 and about 4 months later, I had to leave 82nd Co. and was assigned to Company C 508th Airborne Battalion as a platoon SGT.

In September 1967, we were sent to Ft. Benning as aggressors to support Infantry School Training. I took up sewing to make some extra money because our money was tight and we had to go to camo patches and name tags. So, I made me enough money to live on while

I was in Georgia. My company was sent to Eglin Air Force Base in Fl to aggress against the Rangers. It was ok.

While I was down there three of us were going out to take supplies to the company that was in the field and we stoped at a cafe for a cup of coffee. One of the SGTs. was black but we went inside anyways and we all ordered coffee. When the waitress came back to the table she only bought two cups. I asked where the other cup was and she said the owner wouldn't let her serve the black. I got mad and shoved the other two on the floor and we left. I was really upset about that because James was a soldier just like we were.

It wasn't long before I got orders to report back to Ft. Bragg. While I was there, I received orders to go to the 1st Cavalry Division in Vietnam, that was the first of November 1966. The 1st SGT. who stayed at Benning told me to turn the company operations over to SFC Martinez and catch a flight back to Bragg. The Company was supposed to return to Ft Benning in about a week anyways. I got a flight back with a load of SF guys going to Bragg and called Betty to let her know I was coming home so she could meet me at Pope.

I went to Ft. Bragg to start clearing to go and my orders were canceled. The day I got back to Ft Bragg I reported in the next day at personnel and they told me that they had found another SFC who had been in the states longer than I had so they cancelled my orders and told me I could go back to Ft Benning. I called the 1st SGT. and he told me to take a couple of days at home before I came back. It was nice to be home with Betty and Ricky because I had been gone almost three months then.

When I got back to Benning, I drove my car back. The next day the 1st SGT. called me to the office and told me I had to go back to Ft Brag because they had received orders for me to report to the 1st Battallion 27th Infantry, 25th Infantry Division in Vietnam and would be leaving in December. So, I packed up what stuff I had and turned in the sewing machine I had rented and headed back to Ft Bragg. Well, they didn't cancel those orders.

I didn't want to go and leave Betty and Ricky again because it seemed like I was always going one place or another all the time. I had to get the trailer moved and set up in Maxton for Betty and Ricky. Before you knew it, it was time to leave for California. I arrived in Vietnam Replacement Company and there was a week before I was shipped up to the 25th Div. I was assigned to 1st Bn27th Inf Hq Co as assistant Operations SGT. because the Operations SGT. was going to rotate in January 1967. I got to the 25th just before Christmas 1966 and the Bob Hope show was coming to town.

They were supposed to visit the Bn and eat in one of the companies. They assigned me to escort Mrs. Delores Hope, Bob's wife, because she was always in a different place than he was. It was really nice and she was a very charming lady. It was an honor for me to do it. She was lovely woman. We dined in Hqs Companies dining hall and I was with her for about one and a half hours. I did get to shake hands with Bob and some of the others in the group. I didn't get to go to the show because they put me on duty in the TOC the rest of the day. I did get to take several pictures of them.

Betty wrote me a letter everyday and I always tried to write her a little something. I loved my wife with all my heart and soul and I surely didn't like being away from her and Ricky, but this was my job and it fed us.

Betty (Billy carried this photo with him)

I got my awakening to what was going on in Vietnam. I was assigned as Operation SGT. with the Battalion and saw my first action 2 days after Christmas. I was told I would be on duty in the TOC during the day. The Bn and some of the staff, 1st Bn 27th was going on a mission but I didn't have a clue what it was until it was over. Several of our men had been captured and they went on a trip to rescue them but they weren't where they were told. This happened several times in the next few weeks.

I got to go up with S-3, Major, on an Eagle Snatch. That's when they go looking to capture men to get information. It was my first time flying operations in a helicopter. We were going on a search and snatch operations, looking for enemy soldiers and snatching them up. I was in the command helicopter with the Major and an interpreter from the Vietnam Army.

It was not long before we saw our first 2 Vietnamese. They were carrying bags and word was out that the area payroll was due to be distributed. Sure enough, the bags contained many thousands of Vietnamese money. So, they were runners carrying and delivering money to different groups. The prisoners were bound with their hands behind their backs and blindfolds on. This was the way the Vietnamese use to question prisoners. The officer questioned the prisoners trying to find out where their units were located neither one would speak and the Major ordered me to throw one of them out the door. I obeyed and believe me the other prisoner really started talking.

We were able to pick up lots of small groups of V.C.s. There were about 30 helicopters in the operations. I won't ever forget the screams of the prisoner that day. We were probably 5000 feet high so it was a long scream. I didn't know how I would react at my first killing, whether or not I could really take someone else's life, but it seemed easy and fast. It was quite an experience for me but it didn't take long for me to become an old hand at the different operations that would happen during my tour of duty.

By the middle of January, I had been in the field several times, days at a time. We would lose men to snipers and never see anyone. One shot, one killed or injured soldier. It was frustrating and you began to build up a hate for the VC/North Vietnamese people. Every day it was hot and nasty and you usually didn't get a bath until you got back to the Cu Chi Base Camp. It took me awhile to get some sleep because the 280 mm cannons fired across our area and it would jar the beds when they fired about every 20 minutes.

My first six months in Vietnam were quick because we spent most of it in the field. Exercise Cedar Falls was a nightmare. We lost so many men and never really accomplished anything worthwhile. I saw my first tobacco field in Vietnam. I looked forward to mail call every day because I knew Betty wrote me every day but it was a seven day turn around for mail so you might get a lot one day and none for several days. I knew Betty prayed for my safety every day and I prayed to the Lord many times a day and that is what kept me going. I think Cedar Falls took a lot out of me.

I learned to wash from my helmet, stay awake 18 to 20 hours a day and eat anything that was sent to us. We had a new Battalion

Commander, Col. and he really did have it hard. Sleeping in a chair and eating very little. His language was mild when he first arrived but in the next several months, he began to swear a lot and I surely didn't like it.

After Cedar Falls, we had several weeks stand down and replace our losses. It was during this time in base camp that I received my first Purple Heart. I was hit by shrapnel in both legs trying to reach our motor pool area during an invasion attack, which was frequent and they could come day or night. You never went anywhere without your vest, helmet, or weapon.

I also had to go to Division Headquarters to see what I might get in my second 6 months. They sent us next to an operation with the mechanized armor units on search and destroy operations in the rubber plantations. We searched and the VC destroyed. Sniper killings or wounding one GI at a time. After several weeks with no large body count, we were sent back to Chi Chi.

I remember Martha Ray visiting the Division and she wanted to go visit the outpost on top of the mountain in our area and her helicopter came under fire and that made all the papers and radio. We had troops on top of the mountain and the VC controlled the base of the mountain. Our 280 MM Cannons pounded everyday and it was bombed daily but he VC's survived everything we threw at it.

We got a new S-3 officer, my boss, and he was a pain in the _ _ _ . Between him and the Col., I could lose my cool real easy. They sent us next down south in the Delta, dry, hot, hot, wet crossing (Connell's). After about 3 weeks, same clothes, no radio communications half the time, tempers were short. I recall on one occasion when we got to our night location it was getting dark and we were at an old sugar mill area with a couple of old building frames and I couldn't raise our relay station on the radio, and the Major told me to get on top of the building. I didn't really feel like moving but I knew we had to make contact to let them know where we were so they could send in our night equipment (claymores and food). I finally made it up the wall with a lot of help, but the Major was in a cussing mood and he continued to curse and then he started cursing me. I finally made contact and let them know our location and the Major was still having a fit. I picked up the radio and threw it at him, missing him by inches and if it had hit him, I might have killed him. It sure did get him out of my face for a while anyways. When the choppers brought the night gear it got me a ride back to base camp to separate the two of us for a while and I was able to get clean clothes and a bath.

It was very hot, tiresome, and we were continually sprayed with chemical defoliage while in the Delta. There were plenty of sugarcane and pineapple fields there. The morning I came back out, we swept one of the pineapple fields and the SGT. who was in charge of our security saw a typewriter and went over and tried to pick it up and it was booby trapped and a piece of the steel put his eye out. It made me sick and very angry. He should have been careful and not have moved the typewriter.

We were having to carry 2 canteens of water because it was so hot. That evening as we were setting up our night positions near a large canal one of the guys assigned to protect us was checking out the area by the canal. You couldn't see the canal for the growth of small bushes, and I heard him firing his weapon. So, I grabbed my shotgun and ran in the direction of the firing, when I got to the canal he was standing "frozen" and a VC had a lead on him and I pointed the shotgun and pulled the trigger and it blew his head clear off his shoulders and the VC on the rear of the sampan jumped into the canal and tried to escape because of the bend in the canal I could only see part of him, but I shot always and I heard him holler. By the time I got to the bend, he had exited the bank on the far side. I didn't see him but I heard him moaning in pain, so I jumped in the canal and went to the far bank, climbed out, and headed out on his trail. After about 50 yards, I realized I had shot all my ammo in the shotgun and I started to reload and all the shells were wet from the canal crossing, so I high tailed it back to the canal and there was a crowd there so I was safe.

I didn't sleep very good that night because I would see the man's head doing all kinds of things in my dreams. It is not easy to shoot someone, that's for sure. A day or so later Peter Jennings visited us with his camera crew and they wanted me to jump in the canal again but I told them I was not interested. Later that day after he left us, we heard his chopper came under fire and he was injured.

We were in the Delta almost a month and a half before we had to stand down at Chi Chi. I also remember while we were on the mission we would do a lot of night marches, surround villages at night, letting no one out, and searching the village the next morning looking for VC's. I always wore a red bandana and white socks and our new S-3 officer, Major said at night my socks were aiming points for the VC snipers. He couldn't see at night, so they put a white piece of plastic on my pack so he could see it, another aiming point for the VC snipers. But we both made it. They were bad shots.

I put in for a job with Division G-3 on my second six months of the tour. I went to Hawaii on R & R and met Betty and Ricky for 5 days. They sure did pass fast but it was a much needed break from the war in Vietnam. We had a ball those five days because we knew the Island because we were there from 1962-1965 with 1st Brigade 25th Inf Division. I believe we ate steaks at *Jack's Steakhouse* each night while we were there.

It was a sad moment to have to go back to Vietnam. The plane trip back was very quiet. When I got back, I was assigned to Division G2. Our job, me, a captain and a Sp-4 was to plot targets for the Air Force so they would have a place to drop their ordinance (bombs). A convoy would leave Saigon one day and travel to Tay Ninh and back to Saigon the next day carrying supplies and dropping them along the way. Air cover was required while the convoy was on the roads and that was about 10-12 hours each day. I had a telephone hook up with all the different units from Saigon to Tay Ninh and they would give me targets to hit and I would have to clear them and give them to the Air Force personnel to direct the targeting each day.

I guess I would work an average of 18 hours per day, doing this but my last six months surely did pass by fast. I did get in some flying time with the Air Force FAC pilots. It was something the first time I was up in the small plane and we marked targets for the fighters. The pilot scared me half to death. After the first one the others came routine except when we would draw fire from the ground because there was no place to hide up there. Only once was I up and the plane was hit on one of the wings, but thank God it was not a problem. It made you want to sit on your helmet up there.

Billy in his uniform

When I rotated back to the states, I came back through the hospital route. I developed a hernia on my right side and it wouldn't go away so I only had about 2 weeks left on my tour so the doctors sent me to the field hospital in Saigon and the day I left Chi Chi Hospital was hit that night and several GI were killed, so I escaped that killing field. I was sent from the hospital in Saigon to the 106th General Hospital in Tokyo, Japan. I was there for about three weeks and was sent to the Hold Company at Ft. Bragg, NC.

After my release, I was assigned to Ft. McClellan Ala. We went there in January 1968, and I was assigned as the Post Operations

SGT. and was promoted to MSG E-8. At Fort McClellan at the time was the Chemical School for the Military Police School and the WAC training center and the 141st Transportation Battalion. It didn't take me long to fit right in because I had an outstanding group of officers and NCOs to work with. I helped set up activities for the children on the post, little league baseball, and a lot of other sporting events to give our children something to do besides go to school.

I remember once our pilots were going to make a trip to Washington DC to take some important papers and they asked me if I would like to ride along with them. I was interested in going, but the morning we were supposed to leave, 3rd Army Hg's called and said they were sending several officers to McClellan and wanted me to brief them and show them around. So, I called the airfield and told them I had to cancel out and they asked me if anyone else would like to go and the Controller (a civilian) said he would like to ride with them so he left with them instead of me and due to the timing they didn't change the flight info which had my name on it. Well, about 20 miles from Washington, DC something went wrong with the aircraft and it crashed, killing the two pilots and the controller. We really had to do some fast paperwork because the controller was a civilian and not on the main list and my name was on the manifest, but we did. Again, I had been saved by the Grace of God.

In October 1969, I got orders to go back to Vietnam. This time with the 1st Cav Division. I moved Betty and Ricky back to Maxton and off to Vietnam arriving in the country about the 21st or so of October 1969. I tried to get my orders changed to the 25th Division, but they wouldn't change them so off to the 1st Cav I went not knowing what to expect. I was assigned S-3 SGT. to 2 Bde 1st Cav Division and the unit had just moved forward to L2 Buttons next to Song Be.

When I arrived, the Op SGT. had his handbag packed and left on the same chopper I got off of. I knew something was wrong. (While waiting to go to the brigade I spent a couple of nights in the area studying maps and drawing my field equipment. One night at the

NCO Club I started playing the slot machines with another SGT. and winner takes all, and I surely was lucky and I won several hundred dollars before the night was over, so I said my luck was still with me.)

When I got to L2 Buttons, it had rained and boy what a muddy mess. The Engineers were busy trying to set up an outer bunker line and the weather was not cooperating with them. The first night I slept in a 48 culvert with sandbags on it, a fold up bunk and had to crawl over three bunks to get to an empty one. So one went out at night when you got into bed. I had been having bad headaches for several days and they would make me sick on my stomach.

The next morning after a fine field breakfast, a meeting with the 1st SGT. of Hg Co I was given different sleeping quarters, but not as safe, but at least could get in and out of bed better even if it was the top bunk in a four man made hutch. I went to the aid station for some relief from my headaches and they gave me a shot and that helped some but the next day they sent me to Ben Hau to let a doctor look at me. I saw the doctor and he wanted me to spend a few days at the hospital so they could try and find out the cause, but I told him I wanted to get back to L2 Buttons so he gave me some strong medicine, what I don't know and I didn't care and I caught the first chopper back to Buttons arriving about dark.

I remember eating a good supper, checking at the TOC and then going to lay down. It was raining really good and had been for about all day. The others were already in bed and one of the SGTs. had come up when I did. He was assigned S-2 SGT. and I knew we would be working very closely the next few months. After a little small talk, I climbed into bed, pulling my boots off but not my clothes. That was November 1, 1969.

Well, I had just dozed off and heard rounds coming into the camp, and even though they told me they got shelled nightly, jumped out of bed and I started for the Berm (Bunkers on the perimeter of the base) to take better cover. It was raining cats and dogs and a SGT. went to the Radar Bunker and one bunker had been hit and I heard cries coming from inside so I went inside and two men were wounded and on the ground.

I looked out the port and I could see movement in the wire. I gave my 45 pistol to one of the men and asked for his M16 Rifle and ammo and grenades. The inside of the bunker was a mess but I was able to locate the weapon and ammo and I started shooting - VC were already thru the wire but I kept killing them one at a time, many on the side of the Berm. One time as I leaned out the bunker to fire, a grenade went off and my arms were hit pretty bad but I knew I had to keep firing and no one came to help.

I must have fired a thousand rounds of ammo before they threw a grenade in the bunker. I jumped on it because I knew the two men in the bunker were hurt bad. It didn't go off. So, I put my hand on it and threw it out of the bunker and it hit a VC with a charge across his chest and blew him in half. Later I saw his upper body inside the perimeter. It was a hell of a fight and I guess I was too scared to quit. I had put mud on my arm to stop the bleeding and both the men in the bunker never said anything to me.

As daylight began to come I could hear other GI's coming to the bunker lines but all the VC firing had ceased. They counted 53 dead. I was shocked but said I couldn't have killed them all by myself, but no one else was there and I am sure they didn't kill themselves. All the stories that were written I let the Major do the talking and went about my duties and got my arm and neck cleaned up. The VC sappers did not attempt to get into fire support Buttons again. I was later given the Silver Star for my action and was told I was being put in for the Distinguished Service Cross, but that was never done because I have never received one.

I lost several good friends while at Buttons and I also saw more action at Fire Support Base Brown. The VC's tried to overrun it and I was there also on a mission for the Brigade Commander and the base was hit with grenades and mortar fire and they took a lot of casualties so I sent the wounded out on my chopper and I remained there overnight and boy what a night. No sleep, firing most of the night and at daylight bodies were everywhere outside the fence. It was a scary feeling just to see how many humans lost their lives and for what?

The 2nd Brigade 1st Cav was also the one to find all the large caches of weapons in Cambodia. I didn't go across the border but was at the Command Post helping direct traffic during the operations. The happiest day was the day my replacement came. I left the next morning and for the next couple of days in the country I was next to a bunker. I just wanted to get out alive and back to my family.

When I came back, there was no thank you GI or anything to tell me what a brave thing to do, go fight for your country. Vietnam was a thankless war and today I still wonder why we went to war to lose the thing. 55,000 plus men and women lost their lives and many times more lost their spirit and were wounded beyond every belief. It was a failure from the day it started with no clear objective, goal or sign of success, just political. But a soldier had to go and do what the top says. We were put in harm's way to please the politicians at the time.

In May I think, 1970, I went to Hawaii again to be with Betty and Ricky on R & R. I also had a 30-day leave back to the states. The 13 months passed fast and I was back in the states with Betty and Ricky again. I came back to Ft. Jackson SC and was assigned as S-2 SGT. for the 2nd training Brigade. We still had our small trailer that I had bought in Spring Lake.

Well, this time it didn't take long for Betty to start motherhood again. Ricky was 15 years old and were to have another child and on August 8, 1971, Johnny Woodrow. We had a good life at Ft. Jackson but in October 1972, I was ready to get out of the Army because I had came out on orders again and this time it was to Europe.

In 1972 I was told I was going to be sent to Germany in 1973 but I didn't want to go there. I tried to get Washington to change my orders, but no. So, I put in for retirement in March 1973.

I was put on project transition to Ft. Bragg and assigned to the holding company and I went to work with the Scotland County

Sheriff's Dept. under Sheriff B.P. Lytch. I attended criminal defense training at Richmond Community College and graded 2nd in my class but Libbey-Owens Ford Company offered me a job as Security Supervisor and the pay was $300.00 more a month than the sheriff could pay so upon retiring July 1, 1973 I was working at L.O.F. I had already gone to special training in Toledo Ohio by this time.

I retired from the Army at Fort Jackson, SC on July 1, 1973. Mom and Dad went with us for the graduation, which was a simple ceremony. But I guess for the next couple of days I felt a little down in the dumps. Those first few years at Libbey-Owens Ford were tough for me because in the Army, I wanted everything to be done perfectly and on time and I found out that working with "civilians" that's not the norm. My temper was tested quite often.

My job became routine and no challenge. I started doing the photograph duties and Mr. Hewitt Fulton, my boss, started giving me more personnel work plus we started a monthly newsletter and I was in charge of putting it together, "The Looking Glass." It was fun and a lot of time, but I enjoyed the task.

I got more involved in the Human Resources department doing special projects like awards for perfect attendance, family day - a yearly employee day for fun for the whole family. Christmas gifts, retirement dinners, and more on the job training, photography, and the newsletter that was now four pages, newspaper size. I had nine security officers and was also the go-getter.

LOF became hectic and in 1980 the plant size doubled and our employment rose to 1029 employees and that was a lot of folks. My department included Hewitt, Emily Womble, James Stewart, Randy Jones, Kitty Clewis, later on there were more nurses Linda Currie, Ann Quick, Marie Oates, and Gary Locklear, and Patsy Hendrix, Mary Sutherland. We all worked well as a team.

My health started slowing down in 1994 and May 1, 1996 I was put on disability.

Dateline 1951 -

This is about the time I first heard of Betty Lou Moody. She was seeing my friend, Pat Burroughs and he would tell me about his going out to see her.

1953 - I think...

I was in the Army stationed at Ft. Bragg and Pat was in the Air Force. I remember asking Betty to go to the movies with me. Her father let her go but all the other kids had to go with us. I remember kissing Betty at the *Laura-Max Drive In* that night and she could really kiss just like Pat would brag about. I had not told Betty that I made a bet with Pat that I could go out with her and when I told Betty I think she might have been a little mad but I know her father was very upset and said she wouldn't go out with me again. I think Betty liked me but I didn't see her again until her father passed away and I did visit the family. Later in 1953, I was sent overseas to Japan. I think that one night changed Betty's feelings for Pat.

Myrtle and Reynolds Moody (Betty's parents)

Dateline - 1955 -

I returned from Hawaii in June and the first week at home I went to see Betty again and that was the best thing that ever happened in my life. I lost all my sanity and the love bug hit me hard. I was drawn to her like a magnet. I had never felt this way before and I knew Betty had to be a part of my life until death do us part. When I was with her, my heartbeat speeded up and I became a nervous boy like in a candy store, wanting everything I saw. And I only saw her. Our wedding was simple. I was so excited I didn't pay the J.O.P. and left the marriage licenses and I had to go back and get them. I sure didn't want to go and leave Betty to go to Fort Benning but I was a soldier and duty called.

We were apart for about one month before I could prepare a place for us to live. It was a very small mobile home, 1 bedroom but it was all I could afford at that time and we made it work for us. The park was filled with soldiers and their families like us. I can remember the Kinsey's but there were others also. When we had company over everyone would open up the couches so folks had a place to sleep.

February 1956, Betty got pregnant and we knew we would probably have to find another place to live, so before Ricky was born we moved to a small 2 bedroom apartment about one mile from where we were. Money was very tight and I was a SGT. when we were married but it was very hard on us because I had a car payment during this time plus we bought a small TV and they gave us a small AM radio, which we still have today. Betty was 16 years old when Ricky was born on October 16, 1956, still she was every bit a woman and our love was very strong for each other.

Dateline 1958 -

This would be a 13-month separation in our life and we knew it was going to be hard for us. Mom and Dad let Betty and Ricky live with them. We wrote to each other every day. The ole saying, "Absence makes the heart grow fonder," was surely the case with us. When I came back to the states we went back to Ft. Benning, Georgia and not long after I got back Betty became pregnant again but this one was not to be, she had a miscarriage and I didn't realize how that hurt Betty to lose the unborn child. We both knew it was God's doing and for the best. The price for living was getting higher but our Army pay was not helping us so we always had to watch what we spent, but we always made out. My 22 Cal rifle had helped us quite a few months in our earlier marriage. I was active in sports on post, softball and football so a lot of our evenings were spent that way. We also at one time started going to the craft shop on post and started making some ceramics which we still have some today.

Dateline 1962 -

I knew it would not be long before I had to go overseas again so I tried to exchange duties with a SGT. that was stationed in Alaska because Betty and Ricky would be able to go with me but before we could get approved, I came out on orders to go to the 25th Infantry Division in Hawaii. In June, we left Long Branch California on the *USS Matson Luxury Liner* for Hawaii. Betty got sick before we passed the breakers. The ship's stewardess was very good to Betty trying to help her fight the sickness. We expected to see grass huts and large pineapples growing on trees. We saw fast food signs all over the place. We didn't really know what to expect but for sure the first few days we found out it was no different than where we were except prices were higher and we were surrounded by water. The first several months we were in a hotel until I was able to find a house we could afford to rent. Betty was scared to death of the lizards and mongooses but she managed to avoid them. I started to drink too much and when I went to the big Island of Hawaii on Field training in January 1963, I quit drinking forever.

Betty started saving our money and we still had a good time together going to the beaches on the weekend, cooking commissary hamburgers and playing penny poker with the Kings, Denham's, and David and Candy. We also met Ed and Jeanette Carpenter there and our times were fun and happy. We got quarters on post and Betty and the wives in the block became friends because we did a lot of training while I was there and we were apart a lot. Being apart made our time together so much better. We did not do anything to prevent us from having another child, but it just didn't happen. God had our lives planned but we didn't realize it at the time because the next six years after we returned to the states was very hard on us.

I was supposed to report to Ft. Jackson, SC but they changed my assignment to the 82nd Airborne Division at Ft. Bragg. We bought a home in Laurinburg, NC and resided there for nine months and the training and driving didn't leave me much time with Betty and Ricky. So, I sold my home and bought a mobile home in Spring Lake, NC just off the post at Fort Bragg. Ricky was uprooted again from another school, which would become a part of his young life.

Dateline 1967 -

I was sent to Vietnam in December 1967 and I went to the 1st BN 27th Inf Bn, 25th Inf Div as an Operations SGT. I had been promoted at Ft. Bragg to SGT. 1st class (SFC). I arrived at the Division on the 22nd of December and the Bob Hope Show was in town so I was assigned to escort Mrs. Delores Hope while she was in the Bn area, and it was an honor for me to do it. She was a lovely woman.

I wrote Betty every day that I was able to but times were impossible because of the field duty and the weather during the rainy season. I think it was around June that I got R & R and met Betty for 5 days in Hawaii. We had a wonderful time together and it sure was hard to get back on the plane for Vietnam. I tried to work until I would go to sleep, wake up, work and sleep for the next six months. It passed by fast because I didn't have to go back in the field. December 1968 I returned to Ft. McClellan also and the post G-3 SGT. I had been promoted to Master SGT. E-8. At Ft. McClellan, the US Army women's corp. was training and the Army Chemical School was there, also the Military Police Training Center.

Betty could not understand my working with women and was very jealous of every time I had to work late. It was not pleasant for me, but I tried to get the post to start activities for children and I got in it to help the time pass. In October 1969, I was sent to Vietnam again with the 1st Cav Division, 2nd Brigade. It was hell everyday I was there because of our location we were shelled every day. They tried to overrun our Base camp shortly after I arrived there on November 2, 1969 but we stopped them. In May I think, 1970, I went to Hawaii again to be with Betty and Ricky on R & R. I also had a 30-day leave back to the states.

The 13 months passed fast and I was back in the states with Betty and Ricky again. This time we were at Ft. Jackson, SC. We still had our small trailer that I had bought in Spring Lake. Well, this time it didn't take long for Betty to start motherhood again. Ricky was 15 years old and we were to have another child and on August 8, 1971, Johnny Woodrow. We had a good life at Ft. Jackson but in October 1972, I was ready to get out of the Army because I had come out on orders again and this time it was to Europe. I didn't want to go so I put in my papers to retire.

I put in to go on project transition and I moved to Wagram and worked with the Scotland County Sheriff's Department. In May, I started training with Libbey Owens Ford as Security Supervisor. I was also a volunteer with the Wagram Fire Department.

Betty wanted a girl so we started planning for another child. The place I bought in Wagram I put a doublewide mobile home on it and then built Ricky a large room and a large back porch. On June 28, 1975, Jennifer was born and that completed Betty's dreams of having a daughter. I spent a lot of time away from Betty and the children doing volunteer work and finally in November, 1977 we moved to Maxton. I gave up all my volunteer work and I surely did feel better and not so tired all the time. I guess my way was to always be involved in everything and do it mostly by myself.

LOF became hectic and in 1980 the plant size doubled and our employment rose to 1029 employees and that was a lot of folks. I got more involved in the Human Resources department doing special projects like perfect attendance, family day, Christmas, retirement dinners, photography, and the newsletter that was now four pages, newspaper size. I had nine security officers and was also the go-getter.

Dateline 1986 -

My left knee began to give me problems and in July I had arthroscopic surgery but that only eased the pain for a few months and in December I was on crutches and they didn't want me to go to the plant on crutches. Dec. 16, Dr. Ellis, Moore County, operated on the left knee and replaced it with an artificial joint and after mending I was back to work.

Dateline 1994 -

I was moving tables after one of our training classes and I moved wrong and hurt my back. I couldn't hardly walk. Dr. Shupeck was my doctor in Moore County. He and Dr. Ellis checked to see if it might be my hip but that was ruled out so in November I was operated on. I was told I had degenerative back disease and I would only get worse as time went by. In April 1995, my left knee would not stay in place so I had to be operated on again for that and to make matters worse I had a stroke before I left the hospital, which affected my eyesight somewhat. I also found out that I had gallstones and my gall bladder had to be removed. In October 1995, I went out on six months pay because I was being put on disability retirement from LOF. In February 1996, I found out that I was diabetic. In May 1996, I was put on 100% disability from LOF and I also got disability from Social Security so pay wise I was all right. In June 2000 I was put on regular retirement from LOF and my pay dropped $800.00 per month so we had to tighten our belts some. In June 2000, Betty was put in the hospital in Florence, SC. She had a busted blood vessel in her head and it affected her eyesight. She still has problems and has not driven a vehicle since she went to the hospital.

We thank the Lord every day of our lives and know He will take care of us.

Thank God for Betty and all the wonderful years we have had together and I pray there will be many more -

I know there are many things that have been left out, but my memory is not as good as it used to be.

MSG William R. Ikner Timeline:
  Betty Lou Moody Ikner - wife (married 9-3-55)
  Born: 6-21-35, Whiteville NC to Woodrow and Gertrude Ikner
  Schooled in: Laurel Hill and New Hope, Central, Old Scotland High (10th)

June 1951 - Joined US Navy but was put out because I was only 16 years old, worked one year at Morgan Mills #6, East Laurinburg, NC

June 24, 1952, Joined US Army -

Basic Training - Ft Jackson, SC

Airborne Training - Ft Benning, GA

After ABN Training was stationed with 1st BN 505th Airborne Regiment

HR & HQ Company - 82nd Airborne

Cold Weather Training - Camp Drum, NY - 82nd Airborne Division

Exercise Desert Rock - Desert Rock, Nevada - Operation Knothole

Nuclear Explosion Ground - Troops

Nov 53 - Sent to japan - 187th Airborne Regiment

Feb 54 - Sent to Korea - 25th Inf. Div. 2nd Brigade 27th Inf.

Nov 54 - Sent to Hawaii - 25th Inf Div N.C.O. Academy Instructor

June 55 - Sent to CONARC - Ft. Benning, GA Test and Development (Test NCO)

June 62 - Sent to Hawaii - Hq & Hq Co. 1st BN, 14th Inf. 25th Inf. Div

June 65 - Sent to Ft Bragg - 82nd Admin Co., 82nd ABN Div (Op SGT.)

June 67 - Sent to Vietnam - Hq Co 25th Div - G2 Air SGT.

Dec 67 - Medical Evacuated to 106th General Hospital, Japan to - 82nd Airborne Medical Holding Co.

June 68 - Sent to Hq Co - Ft McClellan, Alabama - G3 SGT.

Oct 69 - Sent to Hq Co, 2d Brigade, 1st Cav Div - Vietnam S-3 SGT.

Nov 70 - Sent to Ft Jackson, SC - 2d Training Brigade - S-2 SGT.

July 73 - Retired - moved to Wagram, NC

Worked at Libbey-Owens Ford Co. - Security Supervision

Deputy Sheriff - Scotland County

Vol. Fire Department - Wagram
Member Wagram American Legion
Nov 77 - Moved to Maxton
Volunteer - R.B. Dean School and Townsend Middle School
1991-1996 - Town Commissioner
May 1, 1996 - Retired from Libbey-Owens Ford Co.

Education:
1954: Korea - Completed Non Commission Officers Course
1956 - 1958 - Ft Benning GA - Completed Army Officers Series 10 & 20 Rescue officer ranking (Captain; Reserves)
1957 - Completed High School GED
1973 - Wagram, NC - Completed criminal investigation course at Richmond Community College

Special Events:
December 1966 - Vietnam - was escort NCO for Bob Hope's wife during their Christmas visit to Vietnam - 25th Infantry Division
1967 - Met and had lunch with actor, Ron Ely (Tarzan) during his visit to the 25th Division in Vietnam
1967 - Met and visited with Peter Jennings and his news team while we were on search and destroy missions in the Delta - Vietnam

Sports:
Ft Benning GA - Played fast pitch softball for 6 years. Our company won more games than any other company within the 3rd Army.
Favorite sport now is Winston Cup Racing - Heroes are Richard Petty (Retired) and Dale Earnhardt

Betty Ikner's Timeline in her Autograph Book:
Married Sept 3, 1955
Ricky was born Oct. 16, 1956
Oct. 1955 - June 1958 - Ft Benning, Ga

Aug 5, 1958 - Sept 7, 1959 - Korea
Oct 1959 - April 18, 1962 - Ft Benning, Ga
June 1, 1962 - May 21, 1965 - Hawaii
Dec 22, 1966 - Dec 3, 1967 - Vietnam
Jan 68 - Oct 9, 1969 Ft. McClellan, Ala.
Oct 10, 1970 - Ft Jackson, SC

Medals

Decorations, Medals, Badges, Commendations, Citations and Campaign Ribbons Awarded

Good Conduct Medal (5th Award)
    Bronze Star Medal (2nd OLC)
    Silver Star
    Purple Heart (1 OLC)
    Army Commendation Medal
    Combat Infantryman's Badge (1 OLC)
    Vietnam Service Medal
    Parachutist Badge
    Korean Service Medal
    Vietnam Campaign Medal with DVC60
    Vietnam Cross of Gallantry with SS&BS
    Armed Forces Honor Medal
    Air Medal (1 OLC)
    4 O/S Bars

William Richard Ikner Sr.

Maxton

William Richard "Billy" Ikner Sr., 71, of Maxton, died April 19, 2007.

No services are planned at this time.

Ikner was born on June 21, 1935, in Columbus County.

He proudly served his country in the United States Army with 21 years of service, which included two tours of duty both in the Korean and Vietnam wars. William was employed with L.O.F. Glass Company as a security supervisor for more than 20 years.

The family said: "He was a loving, caring, special person to all his family and friends and was greatly loved. Heaven has gained a sweet-natured soul and a special angel. Good-bye to our beloved Boopa."

He was preceded in death by his parents, Woodrow and Gertrude Ikner.

Surviving are his loving wife of 51 years, Betty Lou Moody Ikner; two sons, William Richard "Ricky" Ikner Jr. and his wife, Debbie, of Laurinburg, and Johnny W. Ikner and his wife, Tammy, of Hertford; a daughter, Jennifer Lynn Lowry and her husband, Bernard, of Rowland; three grandchildren, April Ikner and Jessica Friede, both of Southern Pines and Solomon Lowry of Rowland; four great-grandchildren, Cole and Nicolas Durand, Payshance and Rachel Friede; two sisters, Rosa Lee Thompson of Laurinburg and Annette Skinner of Hickory; a brother, Carl Ikner of Laurinburg; and a host of family and friends.

Memorials may be made to the American Legion Post No. 0117.

Betty Lou Ikner

Betty Lou Moody Ikner, "Booma" of Maxton, went home to be with her Lord on March 7, 2010.

No services are planned at this time.

Betty was born April 2, 1940, in Robeson County. She was the daughter of Reynolds and Myrtle Moody. A dedicated homemaker, mother, and wife of 53 years.

She was preceded in death by her late husband, William Richard Ikner.

Betty leaves to cherish her memory, her three children, William Ikner Jr. and wife Debbie, both of Laurinburg, Johnny Ikner and wife Tammy, both of Maxton, and Jennifer Ikner Lowry and husband Tres, both of Rowland; her grandchildren, April Ikner, Jessica Friede and husband Adam, Solomon and Samuel Lowry; and great-grandchildren, Cole and Nicolas Durand, Isabella Tracy, Rachel, and Payshance Friede.

She is also survived by brothers, Bobby Moody and wife Linda, and Buddy Dodson all of Maxton; sisters, Dorothy Moody of Maxton, and Mary Jo Jackson of Georgia; and a host of loving family.

Betty was a gentle and loving soul who was loved by everyone who knew her. We will all miss our beloved "BOOMA." The angels in heaven must be rejoicing. As a memoriam to Betty, the family would like to ask that you do her just one favor, if you smoke quit now, don't wait until it is too late.

About the Author

William Richard Ikner, Sr. was a loving husband, father, grandfather, and friend. He was our hero. A day does not go by when we don't think of him and try our best to honor his memory.

We hope the charity work this book can support will help to do that. To learn more about Children of Fallen Heroes, visit their website: https://www.childrenoffallenheroes.org/ and follow them on Facebook.

www.ingramcontent.com/pod-product-compliance
Lightning Source LLC
Chambersburg PA
CBHW062154100526
44589CB00014B/1841